BECOMING

the

BEST VERSION

of

YOURSELF

using
INTENTIONAL
EMPOWERMENT

by
Gladys Latimer Wiggins

Page Layout and Design:

Philip Barnes

Riverducks Design

ISBN: 978-1-958174-00-5

Dedicated to my Grandsons

"And God said, let us make man in our image, after our likeness."
~ Genesis 1:26.

Image refers primarily to mans' spiritual resemblance (rationally and morally) to his maker. We will never be totally like God because He is our creator. Our best hope is to reflect His character in our lives: love, patience, forgiveness, kindness, and faithfulness.

God invested you with full authority to manage your life. He empowers you to make right choices and decisions. You are His agent on earth to make sure His will is done. Continue to use the power within you to make choices that are pleasing to God.

Your worth on earth comes from being made in God's image. With that knowledge you can feel positive about yourself and feel free to love God, know Him personally and make a positive difference in the lives of others.

You are awesome, and you are loved.

Your Grandmother

Table of Contents

Be a good listener

Know when to say "no"

Love everyone

You do not have to "go it alone"

Need advice

Peer pressure

Become your own best friend

*Several sources were used in this book. The sources are listed in the References.

Introduction

Growth and development progress in an orderly sequence from birth to old age. Physical, social, and intellectual development are rapid and fueled by good nutrition, physical activity, human interactions and nurturing parents. The development of a healthy psychological/emotional state is oftentimes left to chance and becomes the by-product of the other areas of development. In fact, values and emotional disposition are typically passed from parents to child.

This interactive book is designed to foster growth and development of the psychological/emotional dimensions of middle school age youth and beyond. In order to maximize benefits, parental participation is encouraged. This book may also be used as a discussion guide for those mentoring or leading youth groups. It has the potential to be transformative in the life of young people.

In this challenging and troubling world, developing a positive psychological state can be an uphill battle. It is frequently stated that a positive attitude is key to successfully managing the ups and downs of life and that your attitude affects other people. Charles Swindoll has said "The remarkable thing is we have a choice everyday regarding the attitude we will embrace for that day." It is not what happens to you that makes the difference. It is how you handle what happens to you. We make our choices, and our choices turn around and make us! A good choice may help move you to a higher level along your journey, while a bad choice may stay with you forever and prevent you from moving forward.

Oftentimes in life we are faced with circumstances beyond our control. It may be a classmate who likes to bully, a stern-faced teacher, or a mean, grouchy neighbor. We cannot control people, facial features, or how long we will live. However, we can control the quality of the years we live and our response to people. We can also control our attitude.

It is a waste of valuable time to focus on things that are outside of your control, and it is wise to expend energy on things that are within your control. So why not choose to enhance the development of positive character qualities like an attitude of gratitude, patience, kindness, positivity, respect, anger control and other favorable qualities. This interactive book provides information on selected positive behaviors and encourages the user to focus on developing or strengthening traits or behavior that may contribute to a life of harmony, wellness, balance and success.

We possess great inner power that can be engaged/activated to develop or strengthen a character trait, habit, or behavior. The user will activate the power within and upon completing the readings and activities, will be empowered to be a better version of self. This process is designed to be completed in twelve months. Continuing the behaviors developed with repetition over time (habituation), you become better and better, ultimately becoming the best version of yourself!

The idea is to become your best self by intentionally engaging in behaviors and activities that develop and strengthen positive qualities. Accept yourself and love yourself as you work to become the "Best Version of Yourself."

Robert Louis Stevenson has said, "To be what we are and become what we are capable of becoming is the only end to life."

Parents' Prayer

As I care for my family today, be with me O Lord I pray.

Make our words kind and give peace to our minds

as we go about the day.

Keep us safe and guide our steps along the way.

Let your love shine through all we say and do.

We thank you Lord for all your blessings

and most of all for this new day.

Help us to use this day for good

and be a blessing to others.

I have no control over what will happen today.

I put my family in your hands and pray

for you to cover them.

Help me Lord to never be too busy

to be available to my children

as they have need for my attention.

Amen

The Challenge Begins

Everything is constantly changing: the world, life, and you. As you look at where you are in life, embrace the idea of becoming "the best version" of yourself. Be disciplined, be intentional and actively read and put this information into practice. The process of "Intentional Empowerment" can work. Be consistent in your actions and take one step at a time and one day at a time.

Following each chapter, there is a calendar page to make notes and ideas to implement as you reinforce what you read about and responded to in the chapter. You will focus on this behavior/trait for twenty-eight to thirty days.

Proceed to the next chapter and complete the calendar activity. As you continue, chapter to chapter, do not forget what you gained from earlier chapters. Continue to integrate these behaviors into your response day after day and they will become a habit. The last eight weeks allow time to reinforce all content with documentation in the form of journal entries. As you move outside of your norm, what may feel uncomfortable to say or do soon becomes your new normal.

As you begin this journey, it is important for you to believe in your ability to engage the great power within you and live a disciplined/intentional life.

Intend to:

express gratitude

be a positive person

control your anger

be kind

be patient

work hard, relax and laugh

be respectful

have a successful bright future

accept responsibility for my life

write a remarkable life story

CHAPTER ONE
Develop an Attitude of Gratitude

On a day-to-day basis the attitude you choose keeps you on the right path or it impedes your progress. The most important choice for you to make daily is "What kind of attitude will I have today?" An attitude of gratitude can boost your mood and general health and enhance how you relate to people. Regular gratitude journaling can increase optimism. The more you think about what you are grateful for, the more grateful you are. Gratitude is indeed a winning attitude.

William A. Ward stated, "Feeling gratitude and not expressing it is like wrapping a present and not giving it." Begin to express your gratitude every day.

Upon awakening, acknowledge three (3) things that you are grateful for. For example, you may say I am grateful for the ability to say, "Good Morning." I am grateful for my family; I am grateful for a new day; or I am grateful for the fun-filled day I had yesterday. There are so many things taken for granted that someone else would be glad to have. So, appreciate the little things and express your gratitude. Share this with your family and remind yourself of its importance by posting a sticky note that lists things you are grateful for. Update your list three to four times per week.

WRITE a "Thank you" note

Take time to write a sincere acknowledgement of thanks to those who demonstrate care, concern and help to you. This may include parents, teacher, coach, mentor, a neighbor or a friend. Let this become a habit as you grow and move through various phases of life. Over the next year, write a monthly thank you note to someone you missed the opportunity to thank, or simply failed to acknowledge appreciation for their thoughtfulness.

Draft your example here so that the process becomes easier and easier for you. A "thank you" memo in the section "Tools to Enhance Communication and Progress" may be copied and used for this purpose.

Dear _____,

_____

_____

_____

_____

_____

Sincerely,

Keep a gratitude journal

*Purchase a journal or use a composition tablet. Begin to make daily notes about things you are grateful for. "In everything give thanks: for this is the will of God in………." 1 Thessalonians 5:18. Even when things do not go the way you want them to or your parent(s) say no to something you ask for, be thankful for that experience and learn from it. It is important to remain positive. Keeping a journal is a great way to express **what is in your heart and work through issues**. Express gratitude for all things, large and small.*

Make it a game to look for new (un-noticed) and unusual things in your environment/ life. Notice what is around you and be grateful and appreciative. Express these feelings and observations in your gratitude journal. Saying "Thank you" will enhance the development of a consistent attitude of gratitude.

Reflect on this question:
Can you think of an experience where things did not go "your way?"

_____yes   _____no

If yes, briefly describe the experience and what you learned from it. If you need to, seek help from your mother, father or guardian with this activity.

_____

_____

_____

_____

The best of us will have experiences where we feel disappointed, confused, sad, melancholy, even depressed. The habit of journaling may be **helpful in reducing bad feelings** related to events and **sometimes writing your thoughts help you to see things more clearly.** As you continue journaling, you may find some entries uplifting on days when you feel sad/blue. Reading earlier recordings may give you the boost you need. The habit of journaling may *continue indefinitely.* After all, working to become a better person is a lifelong endeavor.

Other actions to take:

Gratitude is a behavior, not necessarily a feeling. What we must work with is NOW. When we lose touch with "now," we fail to connect with the beauty and relevance of our daily life and surroundings. What else can you do to promote an attitude of gratitude?

1. **Practice present moment awareness** – Life is full of simple pleasures that are often overlooked. Strive to see and appreciate the beauty and meaning in each moment of your life. **Connect with your surroundings.** Go outside and feel the warmth of the sunshine, the soft breeze of the wind, the cold air on your face, the chirping birds, or make a snow angel. Immerse yourself in the beauty of the sky, the blooming flowers, or the beauty of the landscape. Appreciate whatever your environment offers. You may choose to sit quietly, close your eyes, listen to your breaths in and out, and feel the rise and fall of your chest. Another choice is to immerse yourself in a sport, a hobby, or a project.

BE PRESENT IN EVERY EXPERIENCE THAT YOU HAVE. For example, when you sit down to dinner with your family, put your phone away. Avoid playing games on your phone at the table. Instead focus your attention on your meal and those seated with you. Focusing on your family members shows their importance to you and your love and respect for them.

Try this activity. Put 2-3 raisins in your mouth. Chew slowly and methodically, paying attention to the flavor, the consistency, how the raisins disintegrate in your mouth over time. This is what it means to be present in the moment. No raisins! No problem! Use a bite of any food.

Write a description of this experience, elaborating on your actions and what you noticed about the flavor, texture and consistency.

_____
_____
_____
_____
_____
_____
_____

2. **"Let go" of the past**; practice living in the present – Perhaps something in your life has changed over time. If you remain focused on the past, you deny yourself the ability to **live today**.

If you need to let go of something from previous years or grieve a loss, do so. Continue to remember the loss/hurt you suffered but do not become incapacitated by it. That is, do not stop growing and moving forward. REMEMBER, you cannot change the past; The memories will always live in your heart. It has been said, "Memories are the flowers in the garden of our heart." Over time, you will become more content and feel peaceful.

Think about it!
What unresolved experience do you feel may prevent you from moving forward?

_____
_____

If necessary, discuss this with your parent(s). If there are none, celebrate that realization and be grateful. If there is an unresolved experience or experiences, deal with them one at a time. Use the space below to write a brief description of unresolved experience(s) and solution(s). What did you learn from the experience(s)? What can you do to bring closure to an unresolved experience?

_____

_____

_____

_____

Albert Einstein says, "There are only two ways to live your life. One is as though nothing is a miracle, and the other is as though everything is a miracle."

3. **Give thanks for little miracles** and count your Blessings every day.

4. **Practice appreciation** – Say thanks for common courtesies (the mail carrier, someone who does something for you or offers you a compliment; an offer to help or make a situation better).

Are there things that you need to express appreciation for on a regular basis? The cafeteria worker; a teacher; a friend; a sibling; your coach or parents; food to eat; a home; a family.

_____

_____

_____

_____

_____

_____

"Gratitude unlocks the fullness of life. It turns what we have into enough, and more. It turns denial into acceptance, chaos to order, confusion to clarity. It can turn a meal into a feast, a house into a home, a stranger into a friend."
~ Melody Beattie

Use the following calendar page to make notes and ideas to implement as you reinforce what you read about and responded to in this chapter. Focus on this behavior/trait for twenty-eight to thirty days.

Develop An Attitude of Gratitude

Monday	Tuesday	Wednesday	Thursday	Friday	Saturday	Sunday

a. Write a note expressing love and appreciation for a family member who has supported you. Select a different person each week to acknowledge and thank.

b. Each day, write the name of a person you really appreciated the past 24 hours.

c. Write and post in your view, three things that you are grateful for every day. Don't forget the things frequently taken for granted (walk, talk, see, smell, taste, hear, etc.)

d. Continue to record your thoughts and feelings in your gratitude journal. Look for new/unusual things to be grateful for.

e. Remember to say, "Thank you," "No thank you" and "Please."

f. How did you handle disappointments this month?

This month my focus is:

_____

**Fill in the blank and post this reminder
where you will see it every day this month.**

Duplicate this page for use after completing Chapters 2-10.

CHAPTER TWO
Be a Positive Person

Our values and emotional disposition are believed to be passed from parents to child. If your emotional temperature tends to be toward the hot end of the thermometer, pray for a gentler spirit. Otherwise, let your choice to be a positive person be sincere and from a humble heart. This means you do not have an inflated sense of importance or excessive pride.

The way you think about things has a profound effect on your health. Positive thoughts produce chemicals in your body that enhance the immune system which is important in fighting infection in your body. Optimistic/positive people enjoy life more and relate better to others. Contrast this with negative people who tend to see what is wrong not what is right. They rarely have a solution to the problem, and they complain a lot. Negativity is known to be directly related to heart disease, immune system deficit and decreased ability to cope with physical pain.

Author Anna Quindlen said, "I learned to look at all the good in the world and to try to give some of it back because I believe in it completely and utterly." Learn to **protect your thoughts and fill your mind with positivity**. Instead of focusing on what is wrong, focus on what is right. When you have a challenge, consider the worst and the best and conclude with ways you can help. **Develop a realistic mindset**. This is important because **you believe and internalize what you say and think repeatedly**. When negative thoughts enter your mind, **consciously transform your thoughts into something positive**.

Language is a powerful shaper of attitude and life. The language you choose can shape and influence your perception of things. **By consciously monitoring the words you use, you can direct your attitude** into a **positive channel or a negative channel**. Which one of these statements is preferable, "I have" to call my grandmother or I want to call my grandmother? The first statement sounds like a thoughtless duty. Do you really "have to" do anything? In most instances you do not. Leslie Goldman says, "delivering positivity to others has been scientifically proven to enhance your life." **Use positive direct words** such as want, glad, happy, can and able, to name a few. This is the first step in changing your internal dialogue from negative to positive. Remember, positivity may also boost your physical health.

Be nice to people who may not be nice to you **and let your words be encouraging** to anyone who hears them. Always tactfully speak the truth in love. This means you share your point of view honestly and with a humble spirit. **Choose your words carefully and use a soft voice tone** because a loud voice and harsh words may trigger an angry response. Look directly at the person and be respectful.

Next, when things go wrong as they sometimes do, think positively. Positive thoughts are mentally stimulating. The experience may be an opportunity to learn and grow. An attitude of patience could be the outcome. A positive attitude may not change your situation, but it may catch the attention of those around you. It may even influence others to react/behave in a similar manner. Accept that **things will sometimes not go as planned and bad things do happen. Learn from it and continue to grow.**

CHOOSE TO BE POSITIVE!
Here is an example:
"The law of the garbage truck"

*I got into an Uber and we headed for the airport. The driver was safely going along the roadway when a car suddenly pulled out in front of us. The Uber driver slammed on the brakes, swerved left and barely missed colliding with the car. The driver of the other car rolled his window down and started yelling at the Uber driver. The Uber driver smiled, waved at the guy and continued with our conversation. He appeared unphased by the near collision. So, I asked, "Why did you do that? That guy almost ran into you and could have damaged your car and injured us." He replied, "Many people are like the garbage trucks. They run around full of garbage, full of frustration, full of anger, and full of disappointment." They need a place to dump it and sometimes, they will dump it on you. Never take it personally. Do not spread their garbage to others. Just smile, wave, wish them well and move on. **The bottom line is love people and pray for the ones who behave badly. Life is 10% what happens and 90% how you take it.** Do not let the garbage trucks take over your day.*

"Do not allow yourself to become upset by people or things.
They are powerless!
Your reaction is their only power."
~ Author Unknown

Complete the following exercises:

A. React to the following situations by identifying positive ways to handle them:

1. A classmate called you an unflattering name.

_____

_____

_____

2. You feel like the teacher was unfair in handling a particular situation.

_____

_____

_____

3. You made a "C" on a test instead of the "A" you thought you had made. You were surprised and more importantly, you were disappointed.

_____

_____

_____

4. Your team lost the game after playing hard and doing their best.

_____

_____

_____

B. Think About it!

Have you had a positive outcome after a negative experience/event? If yes, briefly describe the experience. Do you believe your response influenced the outcome? If yes, how?

_____

_____

_____

_____

_____

_____

_____

C. Interpret this message:

OPPORTUNITYISNOWHERE* _____

_____

D. Describe the glass of water by placing a check in front of your response. ★★

_____The glass is ½ full

_____The glass is ½ empty

_____The glass is almost empty

_____The glass is almost full

E. Adopt an empowering slogan such as "Today is a feel-good day," "I will do my very best," "I control my thoughts and my actions," "This is my lucky day," "I am responsible for my actions/behavior," "I choose to be positive," "This is a good day to have a good day." *Write it out and post it as a reminder in your notebook and at home.*

Let your slogan guide your choices. Post notes in places so you can see them when you look in your mirror and throughout the day. This is a way to reshape your view of things around you. You can train your brain to be more positive.

"A healthy attitude is contagious
but don't wait to catch it from others, be a carrier."
- Anonymous

*Two interpretations of the message in "C"

    Opportunity is now here (positive) *or* Opportunity is nowhere (negative)

**Positive response to "D" – the glass is half full

Use this calendar page to make notes and ideas to implement as you reinforce what you read about and responded to in this chapter. Focus on this behavior/trait for twenty-eight to thirty days.

Be a Positive Person

Monday	Tuesday	Wednesday	Thursday	Friday	Saturday	Sunday

a. Begin each day with positive expected outcomes. Write two things you are looking forward to each day.

b. Choose to be positive/optimistic every day. Use positive direct words.

c. Offer encouraging comments to at least two classmates through the course of each day. If not in school, take the same actions toward two other people.

d. Practice being optimistic/positive anytime you are in a "waiting mode" (examples: waiting on a response from mom, waiting for a test score).

e. On your calendar, write one "good" thing that happens to you each day.

f. Give a compliment to someone at least weekly.

You have the power of one!

One positive thought

leads to another

and another.

One step forward

starts a journey and

one spark of hope

lights the way.

And every success

story in history has

happened because

someone gave their

dreams one more try.

Go for it!

- Author Unknown

CHAPTER THREE
Control Anger: Do <u>Not</u> Be a "Hot Head"

Webster defines anger as a strong passion or emotion of displeasure or antagonism. The word anger is short of one letter from danger. It is a normal emotion and a legitimate reaction to what is perceived as unfair treatment or a bad experience. Anger has been described as a fire out of control. It can destroy relationships; be divisive and lead one to make hasty decisions which may cause bitterness, guilt and pain to self and others.

It is not good to repress anger. Repressed anger increases the production of the stress hormone (cortisol) which can contribute to physical illness. Also, when you hold onto anger, you turn a "molehill" into a mountain in your mind and the anger can prevent you from having peace and contentment in life. Expressing anger in healthy ways is important to your emotional and physical well-being.

One way to deal with anger is simply to **let it go and reach out** to those involved. Remember, not everyone thinks the same as you and most people feel that their way of thinking should be heard and respected. Other healthy ways to deal with anger is to **share what you are feeling with a trusted adult, write out your thoughts and feelings, scream into a pillow or use it as a punching bag. You can take timeout.** Petra Kolber says, taking a timeout places distance between your emotions and your thoughts. According to a University of Rochester study, when you are feeling angry, **15 minutes of alone time without electronic devices** can put you in a more peaceful state. Work at trying to **keep things in perspective and accept what you cannot change.**

Lastly, try to **understand the other point of view** and the cause of your anger. Deal with the cause. Taking action to find solutions that are beneficial to everyone may serve to prevent future conflicts.

The outcomes of anger are not all negative. Showing anger occasionally may have some positive benefits. Anger can increase vigilance, sharpen focus and motivate one to reach goals. It can motivate one to fix wrongs seem it society. When managed and used wisely, it can be beneficial and powerful. However, when left unchecked, anger can be destructive.

How Do You Measure Up?

How often do you get angry? _____ frequently _____ infrequently _____ rarely

What do you do when you feel angry?

_____

_____

_____

Think back on an experience when you were angry and write two actions that could have made the experience less hurtful/upsetting.

_____

_____

The key is managing anger when you feel it and expressing it in healthy ways. Work to resolve the issue(s) that made you angry. Hurting someone is never the answer. In the end you also hurt yourself.

SAY NO TO CURSING, YELLING, PUSHING, FIGHTING, NAME CALLING, SPEAKING YOUR MIND, and HANGING OUT WITH OTHER ANGRY PEOPLE.
NEVER RESORT TO VIOLENCE!
It does not help or resolve *anything*.

Remember this! Before you speak, *think* about the words you are about to say and how they may affect the other person. This helps you **develop emotional discipline.** Ask yourself if what I want to say is true? necessary? or kind? Your words can do terrible damage to a person and the damage cannot be undone or reversed. So, choose words carefully and reflect care and concern in your voice tone while maintaining eye contact. If necessary, **take a breather and try a gentle response when you are calm.** These actions demonstrate self-control.

REMEMBER THIS PARAPHRASED EXCERPT FROM "WALKING"

- Author unknown

Walking is good exercise. So, **"walk away"** from arguments that lead you nowhere but anger. The more you **"walk away"** from things that poison your spirit, the happier you will be. Walking outside in nature allows you to calm down and lower the stress hormone (cortisol) level and sunlight increases the production or serotonin (feel good chemical).
Twelve (12) suggestions to help control anger.

1. THINK before you speak and walk away
2. Speak softly
3. Count to ten before reacting
4. Seek to understand
5. Allow others the right to believe or think differently from you.
6. Weigh the importance of the event. If it is of little importance, walk away.
7. Talk to an adult if you feel threatened.
8. Unplug from the need to be right.
9. Appreciate the value of diversity.
10. Be respectful
11. Listen to music
12. Breathe in deeply through your nose and slowly exhale through your lips.

Which of these suggested actions will you try in the future?

_____

_____

_____

Mini Meditation Exercise

In his book, **<u>Don't Sweat the Small Stuff and It's All Small Stuff</u>**, Dr. Richard Carlson shares this mini meditation thought. He combines **counting with your focus on breathing.** Try it when you are feeling a little stress, or no stress. **Use it when you feel yourself getting angry.**

SIT COMFORTABLY AND PLACE YOUR HANDS ON YOUR STOMACH. SLOWLY TAKE A DEEP BREATH IN THROUGH YOUR NOSE (INHALE) AS YOU SAY THE NUMBER ONE. FEEL YOUR STOMACH PULL IN (hold it for a few seconds).

RELAX YOUR ENTIRE BODY AND SLOWLY BREATH OUT THROUGH YOUR MOUTH (EXHALE) TO THE COUNT OF FOUR. Make your exhalation longer than your inhalation. You should feel your body relax from head to toe.

REPEAT THIS PROCESS THROUGH THE NUMBER TEN *while maintaining focus on counting and breathing.*

This meditation exercise **will clear your mind, help alleviate tension and calm you down.** It is almost impossible to remain angry once you are finished. Three things happened from the moment you became angry to the completion of this exercise. First, the intake of oxygen increased. Secondly, your perspective increased (big stuff became small stuff). Finally, your body became more relaxed.

******

If you find yourself getting angry often, plan to improve your response in the future.

Write two actions you have learned about controlling anger that you will use in the future. How will you follow through with these actions?

_____

_____

_____

Share your anger management plan with your parents or another trusted adult.

What are some possible outcomes of angry outbursts?

_____

_____

_____

What is the absolute worst scenario that may result from uncontrolled/unresolved anger?

_____

_____

_____

If you know someone who appears to be angry a lot, consider how you may help that person. Share your observations and attempt to make a difference in that person's life.

_____

_____

_____

Never underestimate the mind-body connection. What are some physical effects of anger?

_____

_____

_____

What are some options for anyone who may have repeated trouble controlling anger?

_____

_____

_____

Pay attention to how you respond to people and experiences you have this month. If you feel good about how you respond and interact with others that is awesome. If not, continue to work to improve so that you are never labeled "a hothead." Also remember to be your "brothers' keeper." If the need presents itself share what you have learned with your friends.

This paraphrased excerpt from Eric V. Copage's book of daily meditations, Black Pearls, sums it up:

We close ourselves to life's possibilities when we live with anger.
We learn to see only the negative and become blind to the positive
like the kindness of people. Relationships with other people suffer.

Use this calendar page to make notes and ideas to implement as you reinforce what you read about and responded to in this chapter. Focus on this behavior/trait for twenty-eight to thirty days.

Control Anger - Do not be a "hot head"

Monday	Tuesday	Wednesday	Thursday	Friday	Saturday	Sunday

a. When you feel angry, walk away, write your thoughts, and think of a healthier response.

b. Pay attention to how you are responding and interacting with others. If things seem tense, STOP and THINK! Consciously choose a more harmonious response.

c. Offer help to a friend or sibling who may appear angry.

d. Forgive the person who made you angry and move on.

e. Plan to PRACTICE the mini meditation exercise three times per week. Review the directions as necessary. Be prepared to use it when necessary.

CHAPTER FOUR
Practice Kindness --It's Free! Be Generous in Giving it Away!

Treating others with kindness begins in the home. Kindness should be evident in the way parents treat each other, their children, friends, and neighbors. If parents are positive role models, chances are their children will treat each other with a kind spirit and the practice of treating people kindly then extends to interactions with people in the community. When you are kind to others, it is returned to you at some time in the future.

When you perform a kind act with no expectations of receiving something in return, it feels good, and it is morally right. Eric Copage states, "Kindness affirms life and our humanity." Practicing kindness is an easy and readily accessible way to spread God's love. The only equipment needed is a caring heart and a gentle spirit.

While opportunities to practice kindness abound, oftentimes we fail to take advantage of them. No act of kindness is too small or too large. Ralph Waldo Emerson said, **"You cannot do a kindness too soon for you never know how soon it will be too late."** Whether you share your lunch with a classmate or volunteer to take your elderly neighbor's trash to the curb, each are valuable examples of showing kindness to another human.

When checking out of the grocery store, the cashier totaled my items, bagged them and handed them to me. She said, "Your groceries were paid for by the last customer." This was a pleasant surprise and it felt good that someone did this for me with no expectations in return. When you are blessed, you should bless someone else. So, on a follow up trip to the grocery store when I heard the customer in front of me ask the cashier to total her purchase progressively because she had a limited amount of money. I seized the opportunity to be kind by telling her I would pay the difference. This is what kindness looks like.

Here is another example: A friend anonymously sends a monetary donation to persons who are struggling. That's kindness. Speaking kind words also counts because words can be a source of encouragement to a despondent person. Practicing kindness can take different forms yet yield the desired positive outcome.

People need encouragement and compassion. Sometimes a compassionate act or encouragement leads to a life-changing experience for someone who is struggling through life, and in and out of run ins with the law. Recently, a news report featured a story about a young lady struggling with drugs and stealing to support her habit; she was arrested frequently, oftentimes by the same police officer. This officer said he saw "something good" in her even though she was arrested repeatedly. He became instrumental in getting her help and transforming her life. She became an advocate for other addicts. Some years later, she saw a news report about a police officer in need of a kidney. She recognized the officer as the one who helped her "clean up" her life. She responded to the appeal for a donor. Miraculously she was a match and gave him a kidney. They became bonded for life. What a wonderful story. One kind and compassionate act led to another and both persons were **big winners.** You never know the impact of your encouraging words or acts on another person.

Kindness is a conscious behavior that can be developed. Practicing random acts of kindness is a way to realize the depths of the reward received from being kind. A random act of kindness gives you a warm, good feeling. Over time it can lead to contentment in your life.

Performing one kind act can have a "snowball effect." The frequency of occurrence grows larger and larger. Kindness can also be contagious. Can you imagine a school where kindness is practiced by most people? Set a goal to **integrate showing kindness in your life.** Remember, when you give of yourself, you also receive.

Create your own "random acts of kindness" calendar. A form in the section "Tools to Enhance Communication and Progress" may be used for this purpose. This will give you a clear picture of how well you are doing. When you are displaying kindness on a regular basis, meaning and purpose in your life becomes magnified.

To get you started here are some ideas of random acts of kindness:

1. Sit with someone you do not know and learn something about them.
2. Hold the door open for the person behind you or someone approaching.
3. Befriend someone who is always alone or may have been bullied.
4. Take your neighbor's trash can in from the street.
5. Use your allowance to buy mom flowers and write her a thank you note.
6. Give an unsolicited compliment to someone. Think about how you feel when someone compliments you.
7. Wash your elderly neighbor's car or ask them "How can I help you?"
8. Forget whose time it is to take the trash out. If the can is full take the trash out.
9. Help a senior load or unload groceries.
10. Offer help to someone in a wheelchair.

Add to the list.

_____

_____

_____

_____

Never forget the power of a kind act.

God created us to be helpers. So, seize every opportunity you can to show kindness. Set a goal to **perform an act of kindness on a weekly basis.** The joy and positivity of a kind act flows in both directions, to the recipient and back to you.

It is easy to be kind when things are going well. How will you respond when your friend treats you unfairly?

_____

_____

Or chooses to hang-out with someone else instead of you?

_____

_____

Your response speaks volumes about your character. Continue to be kind and respectful to your friend. Pray for your friend and your friendship. After all, everyone has a right to feel and think the way they choose and make independent decisions.

Here are ten ways to spread kindness:

1. Take time to listen
2. Give sincere praise when earned.
3. Forgive someone who hurt you.
4. Apologize for something you have done wrong.
5. Do a favor for someone in need.
6. Be polite and courteous.
7. Compromise. Do not start a fight.
8. Negotiate. Do not blame.
9. Put yourself in the other person's place and try to feel what they feel and see their point of view.
10. Problem-solve. Do not tease

- Author Unknown

Lastly, there is a French Proverb that states **"We must assist one another, it is the law of nature."** If you have idle time, immerse yourself in **volunteer activities.** Find a need that no one is meeting and give yourself to it. **Talk it over with your parents** and make it a family affair. Those who have material goods should share with the needy.

What are some community activities you and your family may participate in as volunteers?

_____

_____

John Wesley stated, "Do all the good you can, by all the means you can in all the ways you can, in all the places you can, at all the times you can, as long as you can."

Jimmy Carter, former US President, echoes these sentiments. He said, "My faith demands that I do whatever I can, wherever I can, whenever I can, for as long as I can with whatever I have to try to make a difference."

Remember:

Use your voice for kindness; plan to be kind; help the poor and homeless.

Reflections

Think back over the past year and write a brief paragraph on some experiences you had wherein you were kind to someone. How was your kindness received? How did this experience make you feel?

_____

_____

_____

_____

_____

_____

_____

Secondly, write a brief paragraph wherein someone treated you with notable kindness. How did it make you feel? How did you respond to the act of kindness?

_____

_____

_____

_____

_____

_____

_____

Lastly, remember to **practice kindness daily.** "It is the history of our kindness that alone makes this world tolerable. If it were not for that, for the effect of kind words, kind looks, or kind letters, I would be inclined to think our life a practical jest in the worst possible spirit."

Robert Louis Stevenson

"Kindness is a language the deaf can hear, the blind can see, and the mute can speak."

- Author Unknown

Use this calendar page to make notes and ideas to implement as you reinforce what you read about and responded to in this chapter. Focus on this behavior/trait for twenty-eight to thirty days.

Practice Kindness – It's Free!
Be generous in giving it away

Monday	Tuesday	Wednesday	Thursday	Friday	Saturday	Sunday

    a. Give a compliment to someone every day and observe their response to you.

    b. Make it priority to inspire someone (saying "nice job" or "You've got this")

    c. Offer help to an older person in your neighborhood.

    d. Take out the trash when it is not your time.

    e. Remember, seize opportunities to perform random acts of kindness. Plan and implement at least four.

    f. Participate in a volunteer activity with the family at least once a month.

"Kindness always pays, and it pays most when you don't do it for pay."

- Author Unknown

CHAPTER FIVE
Become a More Patient Person

Patience is the capacity to endure or wait calmly when dealing with delays or situations you cannot control. Many everyday experiences may give good reasons to be impatient. The class clown or the person who disrespect adults in authority may cause you to feel irritated and exasperated when you are serious about your education. The line to purchase tickets for the movie theater is slow and the movie is about to begin. You do not want to miss a thing. What can you do? Stay calm and be patient.

Patience for other people's short comings as well as our own is a desirable quality. We are expected to be patient with each other, making allowance for each other's faults because of your love, Ephesians 4:2. The more patient you are, the more accepting you are to life circumstances as they happen.

Patience is a great coping skill worth developing or strengthening. When you practice patience, it allows time for strategic thinking and decision making. It also helps you gain a clearer view of a situation or what is taking place.

Patience is also a personality trait. Patient people relate to others better, in the home and outside of the home. They have better coping skills. Hence, less stress, a higher chance at achieving goals, better overall health, less depression and anxiety, and more prosocial behaviors like empathy, generosity and compassion. When you are patient with others it shows respect. Patience with family members shows love and patience with yourself demonstrates self-confidence.

We live in an imperfect and fast-paced world inhabited by imperfect and impatient people. We have become accustomed to instant gratification. This makes us less willing to wait for people to respond, things to be done, or tasks to be completed. With practice the quality of patience can be developed and if you set the intention to be patient for a predetermined period your capacity for patience becomes stronger.

Suggestions to develop patience.

To become more "patient" you must be open to **accepting things as they happen**, rather than how you expect or desire them to happen. **Stay calm and acknowledge the unpredictability of life**. The quality of patience can be cultivated with repeated conscious practice. Begin by planning to practice for a set time period.

Tell yourself "I will practice patience today with my sister/brother." I will not allow myself to become frustrated or bothered by anything that happens. If this scenario is not appropriate write another one and describe the outcome after you implement it.

_____

_____

_____

_____

_____

_____

_____

_____

Here are some other practical suggestions to develop "patience" as a virtue.
- Take a walk
- Take deep breaths (calm your mind)
- Count to ten
- Meditate*
- Engage in a creative activity
- Ask for help
- Recognize your triggers

Keep practicing for varied time periods and in different environments that are common to your daily routine. Remember this: ***You become what you practice.***

*Meditation** is the sustained "thinking over" of a subject while sitting uninterrupted, in a quiet place. The goal is to quiet the mind by becoming aware of the continuous chatter and flow of thoughts. As a beginner, meditate at the same time every day and in the same place. Start with five (5) minutes sessions (set a timer). Close your eyes and let your muscles relax. Pay attention to different sounds around you. Take deep breaths, being attentive to the "in" and "out" of the cycle. If the mind wanders, consciously come back to your activity. Continue until the timer sounds. As you adjust to the practice of meditation, increase your time up to 20 minutes.

William Swan Plumer in *"Patience with a Smile"* says, "**Be patient in little things**. Learn to bear the everyday trials and annoyances of life **quietly** and **calmly**, and then when unforeseen trouble or calamity comes, your strength will not forsake you. There is as much difference between genuine patience and sullen endurance, as between the smile of love, and the malicious gnashing of the teeth." **Genuine patience** is an admirable goal to aim for.

On the other end of the spectrum is **impatience**. Some common signs are muscle tension, clenching teeth or hands, irritability, anxiety, snap judgements and snap decision making. Other signs are shallow breathing and feeling frustrated. **If you can figure out which situation(s) set you off, you are on your way to taking control.**

Reflect on recent experiences and describe three situations that led to signs of impatience. These are considered your triggers.

_____

_____

_____

_____

_____

_____

_____

_____

The next time you find yourself feeling impatient, take a step back from the situation and look at it objectively. **Positive self-talk** is a valuable tool to use. Tell yourself to "stay calm," and "smile." Forcing a smile doesn't change anything. However, it helps you calm down and turn your attention to something else that is within your control. Try speaking an uplifting word to someone near you. Be realistic, practical and keep things in perspective. If necessary, let your parent(s) help you with this. **Patience is responsive to self-control, an invaluable character trait.**

Add other positive affirmations to tell yourself when you feel impatient?

_____

_____

Now that you recognize what triggers your impatience response, consciously think of a more positive (beneficial to you) response. For example, if the class clown is the trigger, befriend this person in the lunchroom and try to better understand him/her.

Impatience is somewhat like anger. It is a strong emotion that may lead to frustration, rage, anxiety, and panic attacks. Others may view an impatient person as arrogant and avoid them. With these strong emotions, the stress hormone level increases. This may contribute to physical illness. Also be aware that hunger and inadequate rest and sleep may contribute to impatience. If you recognize either of these as a possible cause, the obvious solution is to fulfill the need.

With an honest assessment of your impatience, you can put into play, actions to move toward becoming a more patient person. Patience as a personality trait can be changed. It is well worth the effort to turn impatience to patience. Displaying patience can **contribute significantly to your inner peace** and contentment. Without it almost any experience can frustrate and upset you.

Patient or Impatient

Which one are you?

_____ patient   _____ impatient

What causes you to become impatient? _____

_____

_____

How frequently do you feel impatient? Circle one of the options below.

Every day   Every week   About once a month   Never

When was the last time you lost your patience? Be specific.

_____

_____

_____

_____

Describe the event. _____

_____

_____

_____

Describe your response _____

_____

_____

_____

What action(s) will you take to become more patient? _____

_____

_____

_____

Capitalize on every opportunity to practice being more patient.

     1. waiting in the check-out line at the store

     2. waiting in line at the concession counter in the theater

     3. The traffic is moving too slow, and you are already late.

     4. Waiting in the cafeteria line

     5. Waiting for your parents or a sibling

     6. _____

Use this calendar page to make notes and ideas to implement as you reinforce what you read about and responded to in this chapter. Focus on this behavior/trait for twenty-eight to thirty days.

Become a More Patient Person

Monday	Tuesday	Wednesday	Thursday	Friday	Saturday	Sunday

a. Choose to practice patience when you must wait! Focus on others who are around you.

b. Three days per week practice Meditation (review directions in this chapter).

c. Choose to breathe slowly and deeply when you start to feel impatient.

d. Practice positive self-talk when feeling frustrated or uneasy by another persons' behavior or actions. "It is their problem, not yours."

e. Take note of events or things that make you feel impatient (restless/ uneasy). How did you restore a feeling of calmness?

CHAPTER SIX
Work, Relax and Laugh. Repeat

Everything is not as serious as we sometimes make it. Laughter and spoken words of encouragement have a profound effect on your health and the health of those around you. Laughter can reduce stress, strengthens the immune system, and promote a healthy heart. It is a wonderful antidote for sadness and bad feelings. In fact, it just feels good to laugh and it makes life more fun and makes you more pleasant to be around. People who laugh together are more productive, cooperative and have fewer conflicts. Remember this: **We do not laugh because we are happy, we are happy because we laugh.** In response to laughter, the body releases endorphins, feel-good chemicals.

Research in this area, tells us that laughter is good medicine. The effect of laughter on the body is similar to progressive relaxation. Some call it "internal jogging." Find something to laugh about every day and spend time with people who like to laugh. When you laugh, it becomes difficult to remain fixed on stressful concerns. Begin to lighten up and laugh at your own mishaps. It can help your perspective and help you realize that everything is not as serious as it may seem. Look for the humor! It will boost your spirit.

One way to begin to cultivate the light side of yourself is to appropriately share a joke or a brain teaser. Be careful not to make others the brunt of your jokes. You can also read something humorous or watch a comical movie or show. Fun and leisure activities give you time-out from important day to day things that are required. Activities like organized sports, a hobby, board games, and jogging are examples of healthy diversion.

Here are a few starter jokes:
#1
One night a burglar assumed no one was at home at this elaborate home in a gated community. He decided to break in and immediately heads to where he thinks the valuables are kept. Suddenly he heard a voice say, "I can see you! Jesus can see you too." The burglar froze in his tracks. In a few minutes, the voice repeated, "I can see you! Jesus can see you too!" The burglar turned his flashlight on and looked around the room. In a corner of the room, he saw a parrot in a birdcage. "Did you say that?" he asked the parrot. The parrot said it again. "I can see you! Jesus can see you

too!" "ah! So what? You are just a parrot," the burglar said.

"I may be just a parrot," replied the parrot. "But Jesus is a DOBERMAN!

#2

Two young boys were camping in the forest one night. But the mosquitoes were so fierce that the boys had to hide under their blankets to keep from getting bitten. Then one of the boys saw some lightening bugs. "We may as well give up," he told his friend. "Now they are coming at us with flashlights."

#3

A minister was opening his mail one morning. Drawing a single sheet of paper from an envelope, he found written on it only one word: "Fool." The following Sunday, he announced during service, "I have known many people who have written letters and have forgotten to sign their names. But this week I received a letter from someone who signed his name and forgot to write the letter."

#4

Mr. Jones went hunting in the woods and became separated from his partner. After walking for hours and becoming exhausted he stumbled into a camp. "Am I glad to see you," he said. I 've been lost for three days." "Don't get too excited my friend," the other hunter replied. "I've been lost for four weeks."

#5

Two six-year-old boys were attending a religious school and giving the teachers problem. After trying everything to make them behave and no positive results, she sent them to the priest. The first boy went in and sat in a chair across the desk from the priest while the other boy remained in the waiting room. The priest asked, "Son, do you know where God is?" The little boy just sat there.

The priest stood up and asked," son, do you know where God is?" The little boy trembled but said nothing. The priest leaned across the desk and again asked, "Do you know where God is?"

The little boy jumped out of his chair, ran out of the office past his friend in the waiting room, and ran all the way home. He got in bed and pulled the covers over his head. His friend followed him home. He came into the bedroom and asked, "What happened in there?" The boy replied, "God is missing, and they think we did it."

#6

A young man came running into the store, panting and very excited. He said to his friend, "Bubba somebody just stole your truck from the parking lot." Bubba replied, "Did you see who it was?" The young man answered, "I couldn't tell, but I got the license tag number!"

#7

An elderly lady took a treasured document in to be laminated. Upon completion of the job and paying for the service, she left. Shortly thereafter, she rushed back in and asked, "May I have my original copy back?"

BRAIN TEASER

1. What can go through water and not get wet?

2. We were born together, and we live one inch apart. We see everything, but we cannot see each other. What are we?

3. What has one foot on each side and one foot in the middle?

4. Why do bagpipers always walk when they play?

5. You mix and disrupt me, but it makes me stronger. You just ignore me, but I get harder over with time. To top it off, it is surprising to see you end up walking all over me. What am I?

6. On a computer keyboard, which vowel is not on the top row of letters?

A WORD OF CAUTION: THERE IS A TIME AND PLACE FOR EVERYTHING. USE HUMOR APPROPRIATELY AND AT THE RIGHT TIME. NEVER MAKE JOKES ABOUT YOUR FRIENDS AND PEOPLE IN GENERAL. YOU NEVER KNOW IF YOU ARE INTERACTING WITH SOMEONES' RELATIVE OR LOVED ONE.

Brain Teaser answers:
#1 sunlight, #2 eyes, #3 a yardstick,
#4 to get away from the noise,
#5 cement, # 6 "A"

Take Time
Take time to **LAUGH**,
It is the music of the soul.
Take time to be friendly,
It is the road to happiness.
Take time to dream,
It is what the future is made of.
Take time to PRAY,
It is the greatest power on earth
- Author Unknown

Think about it!

Do you believe laughter is important to your health?

_____ yes _____no

Do you view yourself as having a sense of humor?

_____yes _____no

Do you enjoy being in the presence of someone who makes you laugh?

_____yes _____no

Do you believe this is a habit you need to strengthen?

_____yes _____no

When is the last time you had a good laugh (event made you laugh out loud more than 30 seconds)?

_____

_____

If this is an area you need to work on, how will you proceed? Be specific in stating your intended actions.

_____

_____

_____

It is important to balance work (school) with rest, and relaxation. Laughter is important to your physical and emotional health. The more you laugh, the better for your health (don't be inappropriate).

Moving forward, adopt this Commitment

I will practice humor (check a joke book out of the library). Practice makes perfect.

I will laugh at myself and share humorous insights.

I will try to laugh every day.

I will choose to watch a comedy movie or video often.

I will explore with my parents/guardian things that make them laugh or cause them to smile and share my goal (find something to laugh about daily) with them.

I will lighten my days by using humor when I feel angry, impatient or at a low place.

"Fruit of the Spirit."

But the fruit of the spirit is love, joy, peace, longsuffering, gentleness, goodness, faith, meekness, temperance... Galatians 5 (22-23).

The fruit of the spirit is character traits which are found in the "nature of Christ." God's goal for our life is to develop in us the character qualities of Jesus. As we grow more like Christ it is desirable that these traits be exhibited.

Match the word (fruit of the spirit) with the definition.

1. Temperance   a. _____   tranquility of mind, freeing one from worry and fear

2. Faith   b. _____   the willing sacrificial giving of oneself for the benefit of another without thought of return

3. Goodness

4. Gentleness   c. _____   kindness

                   d. _____   dependability

5. Long suffering e. _____   self-control, the ability to harness and control one's passions.

6. Joy

7. Peace   f. _____   generosity

8. Love   g. _____   a gladness of heart

9. Meekness   h. _____   gentleness, that is, courtesy and consideration in one's relations with others

                   i. _____   patience with others, the opposite of short temper

On a scale of 1-10, with #1 being "not at all" and #10 being "exceptional," rate yourself on how well you are exhibiting each of the behaviors identified above (#1 - #9). *Anything less than a 5 may be an area to consider for future growth.

1. ____   2. ____   3. ____   4. ____   5. ____   6. ____   7. ____   8. ____   9. ____

Answers to matching activity: a. peace, b. love, c. gentleness, d. faith, e. temperance, f. goodness, g. joy, h. meekness, i. long-suffering.

**"There is nothing I believe in more than this
that laughter adds time to one's life."
- Norman Lear**

Use this calendar page to make notes and ideas to implement as you reinforce what you read about and responded to in this chapter. Focus on this behavior/trait for twenty-eight to thirty days.

Work, Relax and Laugh-Repeat

Monday	Tuesday	Wednesday	Thursday	Friday	Saturday	Sunday

a. Choose to do something that is meaningful and pleasurable on the weekend

b. Find humor in something that upset or disappointed you this month. Write it in your journal.

c. Get in a daily dose of laughter. Choose a time to share a humorous joke or experience.

d. If you have no joke to share, "keep smiling." Your smile may inspire someone else to smile.

e. Plan family game night with joke sharing every Friday.

f. From your response to the "Fruit of the spirit activity" take actions to grow the behaviors where you rated yourself five or less. Be specific in stating your actions on the calendar.

CHAPTER SEVEN
Be Respectful and Respectable

Respect is a positive feeling or action shown towards others. It is also the ability to value and honor another person by showing **care, concern or consideration** for that person's needs or feelings. The definition and ways of showing respect differs in various cultures and for different people. The basic definition above is foundational for this discussion. Showing respect for others is one of the components of a civil society and it provides a solid foundation for relationships with friends, family and other associates. Respect affirms others' rights and worthiness. It is basic to human well-being. Therefore, everyone is due respect by virtue of being human. Hence, we must have a discerning spirit and show respect, but do not emulate or reward people who behave badly and are not law abiding.

Everyone deserves, wants and should show respect. It is an important aspect of personal identity and as stated above, interpersonal relationships. If you do not show respect for others, they will not respect you. This can lead to conflict. Respect can be viewed in a circle. That is to get respect, you give respect. If you give respect, you will get respect. Our mental health is enhanced when we feel respected and when we in turn respect other people. Respect encourages mutual understanding that can contribute to strong connections and positive feelings.

Self-respect refers to the ability to appreciate oneself regardless of what others think. This enables you to respect others. Self-respect is fundamental because you value others to the extent you value yourself.

Respect for others is demonstrated by **being honest, courteous, not putting others down and acting in a caring way with a desire to be helpful.** When you **listen to what someone is saying,** you validate the person and affirm their value and importance. This shows they are worthy of respect. **Serving others, being kind to others, and being polite** are actions that convey care and concern and show respect. Also, when **"thanks"** is expressed, it confirms that we have made a difference and it conveys appreciation and respect.

Self-respect is demonstrated by how we care for our body physically, mentally and spiritually. If one honors himself/herself, action is taken to promote health and respect is shown for others. Here is something to ponder. Is it a show of self-respect for men or boys to wear pants in such a way that their underwear is showing? How would you react if women or girls dressed to show their underwear in public places?

Think about it! Underwear is to be worn as foundation clothing (under your nice jeans or dress). While you have a right to express your individuality, you also demonstrate honor and value for others when you refrain from behavior that may be offensive, like publicly revealing that which is normally private.

Complete the following activity:

List Three (3) people outside of the school environment that you respect? What qualities or attributes of each person are appealing?

_____

_____

_____

How do you show each person that you respect them?

_____

_____

How do you show respect to your teacher and classmates?

_____

_____

_____

How do you view authority figures?

    Trust them _____

    Do not trust them _____

    Have little respect _____

    Respect their position and authority _____

How do you demonstrate self-respect?

Diet _____

Rest and Sleep _____

Activity/Exercise _____

Extracurricular Activity _____

Relationships _____

Self-Improvement _____

Management of emotions/psychological state _____

Spirituality _____

Contribution to community_____

Disrespect

Have you ever been disrespected or treated in a rude/discourteous manner?

_____yes _____no

If yes, write a brief description of what happened.

_____

_____

_____

How did you feel?

_____

How did you respond to the rude/disrespectful action?

_____

_____

_____

Suggestions on Handling Disrespect

First, think before you react so that you do not respond in a like manner. Remember two wrongs do not make a right so do not respond instinctively. Choose to rise above the disrespectful behavior/words and treat it as their problem, not yours. If feasible, explore the reason for the rudeness. Maybe the rude person does not share your cultural norms.

You can always walk away. Maybe the person is just having a bad day. If this is their normal behavior, just tolerate it and try to counter the rudeness with friendliness. Do not change the way you interact. Take some deep breathes and acknowledge that that person's problems are not your responsibility. Always remain empathetic and patient.

"Respect costs nothing"

- Author Unknown

Something to Remember

God created us in His image and crowned us with glory and honor,
having made us "a little lower than the angels." Psalm 8:5
Out of love and reverence for Him,
let us treat ourselves and others with honor and respect.

- Our Daily Bread, April 26, 2008

Use this calendar page to make notes and ideas to implement as you reinforce what you read about and responded to in this chapter. Focus on this behavior/trait for twenty-eight to thirty days.

Be Respectful and Respectable

Monday	Tuesday	Wednesday	Thursday	Friday	Saturday	Sunday

a. Reach out to your parent(s) by writing a love note, telling them some things you love and respect about them. Do the same for two other adults who are influential to you.

b. To get respect, give respect. Remember to be courteous and say "please" and "thank you" or "no thank you."

c. Show respect for adults in charge of you by listening when they speak and following their instructions. Also, those in authority must be respected.

d. Make notes throughout each week of actions you took reflecting respect of self.

CHAPTER EIGHT
Have A Successful and Bright Future

It is smart to set goals for the future. It has been said that "if you fail to plan, you plan to fail." However, God may disrupt your plans with His own plan. As you make plans, it is wise to engage your parents or guardian and seek God's direction. "For I know the plans I have for you declares the Lord, plans to prosper you, plans to give you hope and a future." Jeremiah 29:11

When you involve God, the future is bright. Wherever you go, whatever you do, whatever you experience, whatever challenges you face, God is always with you. He will care for you, guide you and never leave you. Stay focused, calm, and pray.

Do you have a vision for your life? Creating the life you want requires you to make **smart choices** about how you spend your time and what you focus on daily. It is never too early or late to dream about your future. It has been said that a dream written down with a date is a goal, a goal broken down into steps is a plan, and a plan put into action makes your dreams come true.

You are the author of your life's story on earth. **Accept responsibility** for your life and take steps to have a successful and bright future. Remember each new day is a gift from God and another opportunity to grow and progress in achieving your goals, recognize your identity and your purpose in life.

Each Day Is a Gift from God
He has given us
morning brightness, and sun,
Laughter to share, and work to be done.
He has given us rainbows,
flowers, and song.
And the hands of our dear ones
to help us along.
- Author Unknown

Start your day with a series of positive thoughts like today will be a good day or everything will go as I have planned. When you involve only positive thoughts in your mind, they will evolve into experiences that are good. Expect the best and **look for the good in people and everything**. The common bond with others should be "good will." Those with "good will" think the best of others and assume that others have good motives and intend to do what is right. Successful people always look for the best.

To succeed you must **always do your best**. Start practicing good work ethics now by showing up early, working hard and staying late when necessary. Do what is expected, and a little more; give every endeavor 110%. Be a problem solver and not a problem causer.

SOMETHING TO REMEMBER

From a strictly mathematical viewpoint, what equals 100%? **What does it mean to give more than 100%?** Did you ever wonder about those people who say they are giving more than 100%?

You may one day find yourself in a situation where someone wants you to give 100% or more. How about achieving 101%? What equals 100% in life? Here is a mathematical formula that might help you answer these questions.

If A B C D E F G H I J K L M N O P Q R S T U V W X Y Z

is represented as:

1 2 3 4 5 6 7 8 9 10 11 12 13 14 15 16 17 18 19 20 21 22 23 24 25 26

then:

H A R D W O R K

8+1+18+4+23+15+18+11 = **98%**

K N O W L E D G E

11+14+15+23+12+5+4+7+5 = **96%**

A T T I T U D E

1+20+20+9+20+21+4+5 = **100%**

Now, look at how far the love of God will take you.

L O V E O F G O D

12+15+22+5+15+6+7+15+4 = **101%**

Therefore, one can conclude with mathematical certainty that while **hard work** and **knowledge** will get you close, and **attitude** will get you there, it is the **love of God that will put you over the top!**

- Author Unknown

Consider this: "Today Is the Very First Day of The Rest of My Life"
This is the beginning of a new day. I have been
given this day to use as I will, I can waste it ... or
Use it for good, but **what I do today is important,
because I am exchanging a day of my life for it!**
When tomorrow comes, this day will be gone forever,
leaving in its place something that I traded for it.
I want it to be **gain**, and not loss; **good** and not evil,

success, and not failure; in order that I shall not regret the price that I paid for it. I will try just for today, for **you never fail until you stop trying.**

- Author Unknown

Failure can define you or refine you. If you quit, you have allowed failure to define you. If you keep going, learn from it, you have used failure to refine you.

- Author Unknown

A great way to take charge of your life is to ask yourself where would you like to be (education, finances, and personal relationships) when you are twenty-five (25) years old? When you are thirty (30) years old? When you are fifty (50) years old? Dr. Benjamin E. Mays, late president emeritus of Morehouse College had this to say on achieving success. **"It must be borne in mind that the tragedy of life does not lie in not reaching your goal, the tragedy lies in having no goals to reach."**

Age 25

_____

_____

Age 30

_____

_____

Age 50

_____

_____

Write the steps necessary to achieve what you have stated above:

1. _____   2. _____

3. _____   4. _____

5. _____   6. _____

7. _____   8. _____

9. _____   10. _____

Now, make sure you begin to **make things happen for yourself.** This is preferable to waiting for life to happen to you. Make good choices that will move you toward your goals.

Do not forget your support system. God designed your family to be a support system and a safety net to catch you if you stumble or fall. Whoever or whatever your support system may be, be thankful for them. Be patient, loving and respectful.

List all the parts of your life that help **give meaning** to it and serve to **motivate** you to achieve the things you see in your future.

People _____

_____

Places _____

_____

Events _____

_____

Other _____

_____

You may perceive that some things appear to be impossible, but when you **BELIEVE**, you succeed. **BELIEVE you can do whatever you choose.** You have the power. Use this motivating poem to keep yourself encouraged. Share it with your friends.

I CAN

DID is a word of achievement,

WON'T is a word of retreat,

MIGHT is a word of bereavement.

CAN'T is a word of defeat,

OUGHT is a word of duty,

TRY is a word each hour,

WILL is a word of beauty,

CAN is a word of power

- Author Unknown

The difference in who you are today and who you will become depends on you: **your strengths, your weaknesses, what you want, what you do now, your mindset** and so on. Fill your mind with the right things: the best, not the worst, and things you are grateful for. **Go to school and educate yourself so that when your opportunity comes, you are ready. Success comes when opportunity and preparation meet.**

When opportunity knocks, make sure you are ready.

"It is today that we fit ourselves for the greater usefulness of tomorrow."

- W.E.B. DuBois

Complete This Activity:

Make a list of your strengths.

_____

_____

_____

Write the actions you will take to improve your strengths.

_____

_____

_____

Make a list of your weaknesses.

_____

_____

_____

Develop a plan to improve your weaknesses and replace non-productive behaviors with productive behavior. Write the actions you will take. Be specific.

_____

_____

_____

Tim O'Brien offers these points on setting goals:

1. When unsure of your abilities to accomplish the level(s) you have set for yourself, set goals slightly beyond your present abilities at first. Then with each achievement, push your next goal out further.

2. Use moderation and consistency over time to your advantage. A little effective effort each day toward your goals eventually produces significant results.

3. Celebrate your accomplishments with those who are supporting you.

4. You cannot fail unless you give up.

5. If you have a set-back, use it as a learning experience and keep going.

6. Use goals and planning to keep your dreams within your reach

Believe in yourself and your ability to reach the goals you set and do not be afraid to make mistakes. It is a part of learning. If you do not reach a goal as planned, think of it as a learning experience and incorporate what you learned in your subsequent plan. **Celebrate your progress and objectively evaluate your experiences to identify areas you need to improve.** Keep your dream alive.

What is success?

There are many **definitions of success**. The basic assumption in this discussion is that any definition used suggests that as an adult, you are a contributing member of society and engaged in satisfying work that provides an acceptable livelihood. It also supposes you are content and happy. Think about it! Consider the fact that your definition of success may differ at different stages of life. So, what will success look like for you when you are forty years old?

Write it here:

_____

_____

_____

Having a successful life is not always without disappointments. **Perseverance and acceptance of failure and disappointment** are **critical** to being successful. It may surprise you to know that **Michael Jordan's** success came as the result of his intrinsic motivation. It was years of effort, practice, and failure that made him the star that he is today. Michael Jordan said, "I have failed over and over again in my life, and that is why I succeeded."

Abraham Lincoln was no stranger to rejection and failure. He failed in business, suffered a nervous breakdown, and was defeated in his run for president. Rather than taking these disappointments as a sign to surrender, he refused to stop trying his best. The takeaway from these examples is to **persevere**, and use failure as a steppingstone to keep moving, keep trying, keep doing your best. **Success is believing "you can" and always "doing your best."**

PRESS ON

Nothing in the world can take the place of persistence.

TALENT WILL NOT: Nothing is more common than unsuccessful men with talent.

GENIUS WILL NOT: Genius is almost a proverb!

EDUCATION WILL NOT: The world is full of educated derelicts.

PERSISTENCE and DETERMINATION alone are omnipotent.

- Author Unknown

Focus on what you can control and do every day, every week, every month, and every year. Bear in mind, as you move from year to year, it may be necessary to modify goals, timelines or actions. Eventually, you will reach your long-term goal(s).

Booker T. Washington said it best:

"Success is to be measured not so much by the position that one has reached in life as by the obstacles which he has overcome while trying to succeed."

Remember This:

See your goal

Understand the obstacles

Clear your mind of doubt

Create a positive mental picture

Embrace the challenge

Stay on track

Show the world you can do it

- Author unknown

Use this calendar page to make notes and ideas to implement as you reinforce what you read about and responded to in this chapter. Focus on this behavior/trait for twenty-eight to thirty days.

Have a Successful and Bright Future

Monday	Tuesday	Wednesday	Thursday	Friday	Saturday	Sunday

a. Identify two people whose work or life inspires you! Write two qualities that you see in each person that you would like to emulate.

b. Complete this sentence. When I grow up, I want to be just like _____ Why? Have a conversation with your choice person. Tell them about your admiration.

c. What qualities do you see in yourself that will help you achieve your goal(s)?

d. What are your strengths? What are your weaknesses? This month, identify **two things** you can do to strengthen your weaknesses. Practice those **things**.

e. Begin each day by noting at least one thing you like about yourself.

f. Give 100+% in all endeavors.

g. What are two ways you demonstrated your belief in self this month?

CHAPTER NINE
Accept Responsibility for Your Life

The journey along the highway of life is unpredictable. Some days are good, some days are mediocre, and some days may not be good. What kind of experiences may constitute a "not so good day (bad day)?" Here are a few examples: You lost your lunch money; you were disappointed with your test score in science; you were sent to the Principal's Office; your mom was diagnosed with a serious illness, or your favorite teacher was in a terrible accident. You can add your examples here:

_____

_____

_____

_____

_____

_____

The "not so good days" can leave you feeling disappointed, anxious, sad, angry, even bitter. When we **honor God by seeking his ways**, he will give us the help needed for all that we face in life. After all, God does not promise us a life without challenges or problems. He does promise us strength and to be with us through it all.

There will always be challenges to deal with along life's journey and we can always depend on Jesus for help. He will help us get through the day without "falling apart" or saying something hurtful. **Ask God to help you be humble, gentle, kind-hearted and at peace in every situation.** Remember, nothing is too hard for God.

Also **learn to be thankful** in every situation. Being thankful in every situation is not the same as being thankful for every situation. In other words, you are thankful for the opportunity to take the test that you made 70% on, but you are not thankful for the grade that you made. You are thankful for the opportunity because you learned what you did not understand and need to master before you take the unit test. This will help you make a better grade on the exam that carries more weight towards your course grade.

Be a Good Listener

Display God's loving spirit and respect others by being a good listener. Learning requires listening and you can learn from others even when you may not agree with their point of view or action. You have two ears and one mouth, so listen twice as much as you talk.

Know When to Say "No"

In God's Wisdom for Today, Brian Fossett states "It is better to over deliver than to over commit." Say "no" to requests or issues that conflict with your values, dishonest activity, risky behaviors, bullying, illegal activity or if you are disinterested. **Saying "no" may not be easy for some.** To boost your ability to say "no" learn to speak with confidence by looking at the person, speaking firmly and keeping your response short and clear. **Look in the mirror and practice, practice and practice some more.**

What are some other examples of situations that you are likely to say "no" to if they were presented to you?

_____

_____

_____

Love Everyone

When you love one another, the invisible God reveals himself to others through you, and his care is perfected. God loves you perfectly. So, allow Him to love others through you.

- Love the person even if he/she is not your buddy.
- Look past faults or shortcomings
- Do not let differences divide you. Compromise on issues or things that will not matter a year from now.
- Celebrate others' successes.
- Do not be envious or compare yourself or accomplishments to someone else.
- Pray for others. If you are uncertain what to say, pray: **The Lord's Prayer**

> *Our Father, who art in heaven, hallowed be thy name, Thy Kingdom come, Thy will be done on earth, as it is in heaven. Give us this day our daily bread. And forgive us our debts, as we forgive our debtors. And lead us not into temptation but deliver us from evil. For thine is the kingdom, and the power and the glory, forever. Amen*

- Support someone whose voice is not heard (be their voice)
- Reconcile a grudge or grievance by forgiving the person.

- Agree to disagree and move on
- Say only what is helpful for building others up.
- Be the first to say, "I am sorry" or "I apologize."
- Speak the truth with love.

What are some **other ways** to **show love**?

_____

_____

_____

In "The Joy God Provides," Cindy Hess Kasper wrote, **"When life hurts a lot, choose joy. Let your smile be a window of hope, reflecting God's love and the light of His presence in your life."**

You Do Not Have to "go it alone."

Friends are a valuable resource. God created us to give and receive **the benefits of friendship and family**. Everybody needs somebody and somebody is needed by everybody. We need to have meaningful connections to others for encouragement and growth. When life seems tough, physically or emotionally, it is very comforting to know that you are not alone. Do not be afraid to ask for help. It is a sign of strength.

Receiving assistance in life demonstrates understanding of the fact we need each other. Assistance may provide what is needed to persevere and not lose hope. **Never lose hope or give up**.

There is strength in numbers. Dr. James Cross states, "Two are more personally **profitable** than one, more personally **protected** than one, and more personally **powerful** than one. Whatever experiences you may have, **never forget**, "God is in control." He has promised that all experiences will produce something beneficial for you and for God's honor and glory.

The importance of friends and family cannot be over emphasized. **We need each other**. It is also important to remain true to yourself. **Be yourself; be authentic**; be the person God created you to be. Do not waste energy putting on a performance, pretending, and manipulating others. **Do your own thinking and use your brain** to make your own decisions. Nothing is more frustrating than to live your life as someone you are not.

DON'T FOLLOW THE CROWD

Your life is a very special thing; there is no one else like you. For no one born can take your place or do what you will do. You are unique, one of a kind. So, always strive to be yourself, instead of being like the others that you see.

Don't try to be "in" with the crowd or be like all the rest. It is when you are yourself, you know you will be your best.

For God gives each a special call, each soul to Him is dear. But, when you listen to the crowd, God's voice is hard to hear!

- Author Unknown

"The company you keep influences your thinking, thinking influences your actions, your actions influence your character, and your character determines your destiny."

- Daily Devotional: The Word for you today, April 26, 2021

It is better to be alone than to be in the wrong company. You become like those with whom you associate. Some of your friends or associates may not want you to grow. **Choose your friends and associates carefully.**

Need advice?

Consider this: Never receive advice from someone who cannot help you find a solution to your problem or from an unproductive person. Do not follow someone who is not going anywhere. If you need advice from someone on an important subject, seek it from someone you respect who can speak from experience. Someone who has it together and who has what you are looking for. Seek advice from qualified people like your parents, other family members, a coach, a counselor, a teacher, a minister or mentor.

Peer Pressure

Peers are associates who are your age, gender, or share other traits. Peer pressure is when someone in your peer group tries to influence you to do something you may not want to do. Peer pressure can be positive or negative and it can be hard to resist. Everyone likes to be accepted and valued by their friends. However, never allow anyone to pressure you to do things against your personal beliefs. **Choose your friends wisely.** That means make friends with others who share **similar values** and **beliefs**. Make a personal commitment to be a positive peer.

How to Handle Peer Pressure

1. Look out for number one (yourself). **Become your own best friend** and do what is right for you.
2. When an invitation is given to participate in _____, evaluate all options before deciding. Listen to your mind and body about choices to make. They can help determine when a decision may be wrong. When in doubt, talk to a trusted adult or parent.

Evaluate your Options

Positives to saying "yes"   Negatives to saying "yes"

_____   _____

_____   _____

Positives to saying "no"   Negatives to saying "no"

_____   _____

_____   _____

3. Always speak for yourself, politely and firmly (be assertive)
4. Make "yes" mean "yes" and "no" mean "no" (make eye contact with your head held high). Repeat message as necessary. Make a "no" response funny by saying something like "I'm trying to be less popular this year or I don't do that on days that end with "day."
5. Do not believe everything you hear.

Become Your Own Best Friend

1. Focus on your inner talents, skills, character and your heart. You will like yourself no matter how your day goes or what someone else may say about you. **Believe in yourself, you are worth it!**
2. Replace negative thoughts with **positive thoughts**. Pat yourself on the back. Do not be overly critical of yourself.

3. **Objectively** looking at yourself may be instrumental in setting future goals that will help you strengthen a weakness.

4. If your friends make mistakes, **forgive** them. Likewise, forgive yourself for mistakes.

5. Do not be afraid to **share your ideas and opinions. Speak up for yourself** and stand up to those who try to put you down. Always remember, we don't all think alike, and everyone is entitled to their opinion.

> *Not everyone*
> *Thinks the way you think*
> *Knows the things you know,*
> *Believes the things you believe,*
> *Nor acts the way you would act.*
> *Remember this*
> *and you will go a long way*
> *in getting along with people.*
> \- Arthur Ferman

6. List three (3) things that make you happy and that you like about yourself. Do this monthly.

_____

_____

_____

7. Character counts. So always insist on **integrity and honesty**.

8. Accept as friends, those who **love you for who you are**, not what you have or how you look.

9. Take pride in yourself and be the **unique person** God created you to be.

10. Volunteer in community service projects and have fun. Remember when you volunteer, you ***plant seeds of kindness***.

Use the following calendar page to make notes and ideas to implement as you reinforce what you read about and responded to in this chapter. Focus on this behavior/trait for twenty-eight to thirty days.

Accept Responsibility for Your Life

Monday	Tuesday	Wednesday	Thursday	Friday	Saturday	Sunday

a. Remember, you can take advice and guidance from others, but the ultimate decision is yours.

b. What are some examples of experiences when you were your own best friend?

c. Write a list of your physical and personality traits that you are grateful for and post your note so you can read it often.

d. Be an encourager. Use phrases like "keep up the good work," "I like that," "I'm happy for you," or "I am glad that you are my friend."

e. Praise or congratulate a classmate on an accomplishment.

f. Know when to say "no" and do not follow the crowd.

g. Note examples of situations when friends or family were resourceful and when you showed love to others.

WEB DuBois says, "Today is the seed time,
now are the hours of work,
and tomorrow comes the harvest and the playtime."

CHAPTER TEN
Your Life's Book

Life's Book

No matter what else you are doing from cradle days through to the end, you are writing your life's secret story. Each day sees another page penned.

Each month ends a thirty-page chapter; each year means the end of a part, and never an act is misstated or even one wish of the heart.

Each day when you awake, the book opens, revealing a page clean and white. What thoughts and what words and what doings will cover its pages by night?

God leaves that to you. You are the writer and never a word shall grow dim, til' the day you write the word finished and you give your life's book back to Him.

- Author Unknown

Attitude

by Charles Swindoll

"The longer I live, the more I realize the impact of attitude on life. Attitude, to me, is more important than facts. It is more important than the past, than education, than money, than circumstances, than failures, than successes, than what other people think or say or do. It is more important than appearance, giftedness or skill. It will make or break a company … a church … a home. The remarkable thing is we have a choice every day regarding the attitude we will embrace for that day. We cannot change our past … we cannot change the fact that people will act in a certain way. We cannot change the inevitable. The only thing we can do is play on the string we have, and that is our attitude… I am convinced that life is 10% what happens to me and 90% how I react to it. And, so it is with you.

We are in charge of our attitudes...

Three Nuggets worth Remembering

1. *Attitudes are contagious; be a carrier of a healthy attitude. Others may catch it from you!*
2. *Wherever you go, take your positive attitude with you.*
3. *Your reaction to life events is more powerful than the event.*

Celebrate Everyday

Cherish your life, family, and education. There are so many things in life to hold dear to you. List some things you would place high on your priority list.

_____

_____

_____

Enthusiasm can add a spark to your life. Be enthusiastic about all aspects of your life. When you smile the whole world will smile with you. **Try sharing a smile with someone who appears apathetic and unassuming.** See if they return your greeting with a smile.

Live with passion. Make the most of every day, every event, every gift, every relationship. How have you made the most of your experiences this week?

_____

_____

_____

_____

Looking ahead, what will **your passion** be? A strong suggestion, 1 Timothy 6:11: "Pursue righteousness, godliness, faith, love, and gentleness." These traits will **grow in you as you live an intentional life.** Practicing gratitude, positivity, kindness, patience, a healthy response to anger, forgiveness, love of people, self-respect and respect of others, hard work and love of God will enrich your life beyond measure.

Excitement yields more personal satisfaction. Get excited about that project, family events, and other activities.

Believe in yourself. The power of belief allows you to overcome challenges and obstacles that may get in your way.

"What you are is God's gift to you. What you do with yourself is your gift to God."
- Author Unknown

Rejoice or feel and express gladness for the miracles in your life. The ability to smell, see, hear, walk, talk, think, or move. Your functioning body is a miracle and something to rejoice about. What are some other things you choose to rejoice over?

_____

_____

Attitude and actions: Are you a role model for others to emulate? As you go through each day pay attention to your attitude and keep it positive. How did you do this week?

_____

_____

The Gift

"Give the gift of encouragement every day.

Pass it out freely and in gentle ways.

There is no need for ribbons to make it look grand.

Just the simple encouragement of a kind, helping hand."

\- Joan Stephens

Time is precious:

Do you plan and use your time wisely?

Do you work on projects progressively so that you do your very best?

Are you a procrastinator (wait to the very last minute to get things done)?

Time is precious. Don't waste it.

(Now don't misunderstand, there are times when it is perfectly ok to do nothing.)

Let "Murphy's Law" guide you when you have deadlines:

"Nothing is as easy as it looks. Everything takes longer than you expect.

And if anything can go wrong, it will at the worst possible moment."

\- Author Unknown

Imagination: The power of imagination is at the root of every great achievement or change. Take time to imagine!

Opportunity: When we celebrate our lives, we focus on what works and then we can see and appreciate the many opportunities that we have each day.

Now, celebrate life every day.

Adapted from Jeff Herring

"Please don't panic; it's time to celebrate."

http://www.tdo.com

Celebration

"Every day may not be good, but there is something good in every day."

- Author unknown

Forward Thinking Activity

Beginning with age 25, write a synopsis of what you believe your life will look like at that point. Project in 20-year increments.

25-45 years of age

_____

_____

_____

45-65 years of age

_____

_____

_____

65-85 years of age

_____

_____

_____

85 years forward

_____

_____

_____

Enthusiasm

Enthusiasm! That certain something that makes us great-that pulls us out of the mediocre and commonplace-that builds into us power. It glows and shines; it lights up our faces.

Enthusiasm-the maker of friends-the maker of smiles-the producer of confidence. It cries to the world, "I've got what it takes."

Enthusiasm-the inspiration that makes you "wake up and live." It puts spring in your step-spring in your heart-a twinkle in your eyes-confidence in yourself and your fellowmen.

Enthusiasm is reason gone mad to achieve a definite, rational objective.

Enthusiasm is inflamed by opposition, but never converted; it's the leaping lightning that blasts obstacles from its path.

Enthusiasm is the vibrant thrill in your voice that sways the will of others into harmony with your own.

Enthusiasm is the magnet that draws kindred souls with irresistible force and electrifies them with magnetism of its own resolves. Getting people to like you is merely the other side of liking them. If you have zest and enthusiasm, you attract zest and enthusiasm. Life does give back in kind.

Norman Vincent Peale

Enthusiasm -does not come easy to everyone; sometimes, it is not for lack of trying, but we simply are not all naturally optimistic people. However, while negative feelings are valid as positive ones, they can really take over our lives and harm us, in the long run,"

Lucy Stanmore, "Enthusiasm 101"

Use this calendar page to make notes and ideas to implement as you reinforce what you read about and responded to in this chapter. Focus on this behavior/trait for twenty-eight to thirty days.

Your Life's Book

Monday	Tuesday	Wednesday	Thursday	Friday	Saturday	Sunday

a. Believe in yourself and your ability! Remember this powerful phrase. IF IT IS TO BE, IT IS UP TO ME.

b. Find something good in each day and be joyful.

c. When you have deadlines to meet, always plan your time and follow your plan. In that way you will meet the target date and avoid rushing and not doing your best. Remember Murphy's Law.

d. Never leave home without your positive attitude and enthusiasm.

e. Be respectful, kindhearted and helpful.

f. Celebrate life every day. What are some ways you chose to celebrate this month?

CHAPTER ELEVEN
Laboratory Experience ~ Life

Over the past ten months you have worked on making changes that will help/enable you to improve responses and interactions with others to reflect positive virtues in words and actions. Now is the time to integrate the use of these qualities into your life experiences.

Life is unpredictable. Sometimes it can be like a roller coaster, up and down, up and down, up and down, always full of surprises. The older you get, the more often disappointments or disenchantments may be a part of your day-to-day experiences. Unexpected outcomes, accidents, and incidents happen as well as the positive expected outcomes. Usually there are more good experiences than bad. That's the way life goes. You may hear some say, "life happens."

Since you cannot control all of life experiences, it is wise to be flexible and focus on those things that you can control. When you cannot control the circumstances, you can control your responses. After all life is 10% what happens to you and 90% how you react to it.

Your Assignment

Moving forward, be intentional about choosing behaviors that give your life the most meaning, harmony, wellness, and balance. Over the next eight weeks, the focus will be on reinforcing the concepts learned in chapters 1-10. As you go through each days' activities, whether at school, at home, at the park, church or a friend's house, implement actions on the "TO DO LIST," one week at a time. Each week add a focus and carry over as is appropriate, the last area of focus.

We have a predetermined amount of time in each day. How you spend your time reflects your priority. You are encouraged to seize every opportunity to practice what you have learned. While time is constant, day to day experiences will vary.

Over time, opportunities will likewise be varied. Stay alert and motivated, so that when the moment is right you can capitalize on the opportunity. In fact, look for opportunities to practice the positive behaviors. So that you make the most of every day.

As you grow older and responsibilities increase, "time management" becomes more important. In "A Year of Time" by Steven B. Cloud, he says, "Like the air we breathe, time comes to us as a part of life." Time is constantly moving. You cannot change it, reclaim it, borrow it, lend it, or roll it over. When it is gone, it's gone. It is an important possession and should not be wasted. As your responsibilities grow and you work toward achieving goals in life, USE TIME WISELY.

There are 24 hours in a day and 60 minutes in an hour. Therefore, there are 1,440 minutes in every hour. There are 60 seconds in every minute. Therefore, there are 86,400 seconds in every day.

Each of us has a bank of time. Every morning it credits you with 86,400 seconds. Each night at 12 midnight, it writes off as lost, whatever of this you have failed to invest to good purpose. It carries over no balance and allows no overdraft. There is no drawing against tomorrow. You must live in the present on todays' deposits. Invest it so as to get from it the utmost in health, happiness, and success! The clock is "running."

Make the most of today! Yesterday is history, tomorrow is a mystery. Today is a gift, that is why it is called the present!

- Author Unknown

You have 86,400 opportunities to think and speak positive thoughts, express gratitude, display patience, be respectable and respectful, manage anger in a healthy way, treat others with kindness, relax and laugh, show love, and make other choices that contribute to a successful and bright future. To accomplish your goal of becoming the best version of yourself by living intentionally, take one day at a time and focus on what you can do "today." **What may appear impossible becomes possible when you are committed to do the little things that are within your control every day, every week, every month and every year**. With the passage of time your long-term goal will be achieved.

Remember this: "Why worry about things you cannot control when you can keep yourself busy controlling the things that depend on you."

- Author Unknown

INTENTIONAL LIVING - TO DO LIST

Week 1 – Develop an Attitude of Gratitude

* Express gratitude verbally and in writing; Use sticky notes and thank you cards and notes; Stationary options in "Tools to Enhance Communication and Progress" may be copied for use.
* Continue journaling. Make entries daily, preferably at the end of the day.
* Practice "Present Moment Awareness" at least every other day.
* Identify at least three things you felt gratitude for as you walk outside in nature. Describe results in the space below.
* Share your thoughts and feelings with your family on a regular basis.
* Let "please," "thank you," and "no thank you" flow freely from your mouth. Express thanks for your food before eating.
* Share a smile with someone who does not have one.

Notes

_____

_____

_____

_____

_____

_____

_____

_____

_____

_____

_____

_____

_____

_____

_____ continue on back of page

INTENTIONAL LIVING - TO DO LIST

Week 2 – Be a Positive Person

* When you wake up, instead of reaching for your phone, take two deep breathes and set your intentions for the day. For example, "I will do well on my test" or "I will show random kindness to at least two persons."
* Fill your mind with positive thoughts.
* Practice positive self -talk daily. "I will do well on the exam because I studied hard," "I like what I see when I look in the mirror," or "I am pleased with my progress."
* Offer a compliment to at least one person each day
* Choose a positive attitude every day and be enthusiastic.
* Offer uplifting comments to others: "good job," "I like that!" "keep up the good work."
* Avoid negativism.

Notes

_____

_____

_____

_____

_____

_____

_____

_____

_____

_____

_____

_____

_____

_____

_____ continue on back of page

INTENTIONAL LIVING - TO DO LIST

Week 3 – Control Anger – Don't be a "hot head"

* Deal with anger promptly and in a healthy way. Use the space below to describe your anger management experiences.
* Practice mini meditation every other day. By practicing, when the real situation presents itself you will be ready. Describe your progress below.
* Smile – it is impossible to remain angry when you smile; tell a joke.
* Sing a happy song
* Forgive and forget; move on. A "Forgiveness" form can be found in the section "Tools to Enhance Communication and Progress."

Notes

_____

_____

_____

_____

_____

_____

_____

_____

_____

_____

_____

_____

_____

_____

_____

_____

_____

_____continue on back of page

INTENTIONAL LIVING - TO DO LIST

Week 4 – Practice Kindness – It's free

* Be kind to others every day.
* Practice random acts of kindness every day, planned and unplanned. A Random Acts of Kindness Calendar is included in the section "Tools to Enhance Communication and Progress."
* Participate in a volunteer service at least once a month. Remember to make this a family affair. What was this experience like?
* Offer a compliment to at least one person every day.
* Every day tell at least one person something you like, appreciate or admire about them.
* Hold the door open for the person behind you.

Notes

_____

_____

_____

_____

_____

_____

_____

_____

_____

_____

_____

_____

_____

_____

_____

_____

_____Continue on back of page

INTENTIONAL LIVING - TO DO LIST

Week 5 – Become more Patient

* Begin each day with a statement of intent. On this day, I will not be annoyed or frustrated by anything or anybody.

* Practice meditation every other day. Review the process as necessary.

* Practice cultivating patience anytime you are waiting for whatever. When you feel frustration or annoyance, choose a more positive response: singing or looking for something positive in the people around you.

* Turn your frown upside down – Smile

* Through conversation try to understand the person or the situation that caused you to feel impatience.

* Use your time wisely.

Notes

_____

_____

_____

_____

_____

_____

_____

_____

_____

_____

_____

_____

_____

_____

_____

_____ continue on back of page

INTENTIONAL LIVING - TO DO LIST

Week 6 – Work, Relax, Laugh – Repeat

* Get your daily dose of laughter.
* Take a leisurely walk with the family.
* Have family movie night- choose a comedy.
* Identify which of the nine 'fruit of the spirit" you need to strengthen and what you can do right now to become stronger in that quality.
* Complete the "Self-Improvement" Chart in the section "Tools to Enhance Communication and Progress."
* As the opportunity presents itself, respond to life experiences with a "stronger" showing of the appropriate spirit.
* Share a joke with your friends and encourage them to do the same.

Notes

_____

_____

_____

_____

_____

_____

_____

_____

_____

_____

_____

_____

_____

_____

_____

_____continue on back of page

INTENTIONAL LIVING - TO DO LIST

Week 7 – Be Respectful and Respectable

* Respect others and they will respect you; hang out with people who have like values and interests.
* Respect adults by listening and following directions.
* Remember to say "please," "thank you," and "no thank you."
* When others are disrespectful, think first, walk away, take some deep breaths.
* Set a goal to display a higher level of respect for your mother and father. Write a note telling how they influence you.
* Wellness Wednesday – Do something to help your physical health. Every Wednesday, make healthier choices when given the opportunity to choose your meal or a snack.
* Take a family walk or bike ride.
* Be the first to say "I am sorry."

Notes

_____

_____

_____

_____

_____

_____

_____

_____

_____

_____

_____

_____

_____

_____ continue on back of page

INTENTIONAL LIVING - TO DO LIST

Week 8 – Have a Successful and Bright Future

* Show love to everyone who crosses your path; choose friends who love you for who you are.
* Do your best in all endeavors.
* Tell the people in your life thank you for their role in your life and motivating you to stay focused.
* Identify five qualities in yourself that you are proud of. Remind yourself of these often and add to the list periodically.
* Listen more than you speak and let your words be uplifting.
* Look for the good in experiences and people around me, acknowledge it. Make a list so that you can see your progress.
* Identify career choices you are considering.
* Practice saying "no" to hypothetical situations that you create. This is a learnable skill and by practicing, you are prepared when the situation presents itself.
* In a group setting, share your ideas and opinions.
* Use your time wisely. Develop a plan to reflect your timeline for completing an assignment. Show dates and activities.

Notes

_____

_____

_____

_____

_____

_____

_____

_____

_____

_____

_____continue on back of page

WORK WEEK OF A WINNER!

Be kind, patient
and do your best.
SUNDAY

Respect others
and yourself.
MONDAY

Have an attitude
of gratitude.
TUESDAY

Forgive others
and yourself.
WEDNESDAY

Choose your
friends carefully.
THURSDAY

Have a
positive attitude.
FRIDAY

Do something
to help others.
SATURDAY

Deal with anger/disappointment
promptly and in healthy ways.

Choose to see the good in others
and in experiences (positivity).

Relax! Enjoy Life!
Stay close to your family.

85

NEVER FORGET — YOU HAVE POWER

You have the power to take charge of your tomorrow. Close your eyes and see yourself fifteen years from now and twenty years from now. What do you see?

Write it down and enumerate the steps you need to take ... for your future is at stake. This is the beginning of making things happen for yourself.

One day at a time.
One week at a time.
One month at a time.
One year at a time.
Your dream slowly comes into view.

Adjust your goals and actions as needed.
Your dream becomes a reality
if you never, never give up.

GO TO WORK NOW! Take the necessary actions to make your dream a reality. If you stumble or if you fall, get up, learn from the experience and keep moving.

WHATEVER YOU DO, NEVER GIVE UP!
Let positivity prevail.

Glossary

1. acknowledgment – recognition or favorable notice of an act or achievement.
2. admirable – deserving the highest esteem.
3. antagonism – actively expressed opposition; hostility.
4. apathetic – having or showing little or no feeling or emotions; having or showing little interest or concern.
5. compassion – sympathetic consciousness of others.
6. empathy – the capacity for participation in another's feelings or ideas.
7. emulate – imitate; to strive to equal or excel.
8. engaged – being actively involved or committed.
9. exasperated – irritated or annoyed.
10. exhalation – the act of breathing out.
11. expend – to consume by use; use up.
12. generosity – abundance
13. habituation – the process of making habitual; acting in the same manner by force of habit.
14. habitude – habitual mode of behavior.
15. incapacitated – disable; to deprive of natural power.
16. indefinitely – not definite; not precise.
17. inhalation – the act of breathing in.
18. mediocre – moderate or low quality; ordinary.
19. melancholy – depression of spirit; dejection; causing sadness.
20. persevere – to persist in an undertaking in spite of previous discouragement.
21. previous – going before in time and order.
22. procrastinate – to put off intentionally and habitually.
23. reconcile – to restore to friendship or harmony.
24. repress. To hold in by self-control.
25. unpredictable – unable to declare in advance; not predictable.

References

1. Adam Holz, 2021, "The Saddest Goose", April 23, Our Daily Bread

2. Alexander Salazar, 2019, Respect: What is it, types, examples, learn and teach: online cognitive assessment.

3. Amy Boucher Pye, 2021, "The Secret of contentment," June 30; "Seeking God's Help," July 22, Our Daily Bread.

4. Ann Cetas, 2021, Listen and Learn," July 15, Our Daily Bread.

5. Anna Goldfarb, 2018, "How to be a More Patient Person." The New York Times

6. Ann's Newsletter, 2000-present, anniedupree@comcast.net

7. "Are you a Patient Person?" 2018, The Learning Network.

8. Cindy Hess Kasper, 2021, "The Joy God Provides." Our Daily Bread

9. Courtney Ackerman, 2020, "28 Benefits of Gratitude and most Significant Research Findings" positivepsychology.com.

10. Daily Devotional: The word for you Today, 2021, "By the Grace of God," March 27; "A Perfect Heart Leads to a Healthy Body," December 10; "The Power of Influence," April 26; "The Rewards of Kindness," May 29; "Goodness," March 5; "Your Words Reveal Your Heart." March 9; "Try to be Tactful," May 4; "God will take Care of You." May 24; "Bring Out the Best in Others," May 18; "Speak Positively (3)."; "Speak Positively (4)," July 6.

11. Deep Patel, 2019, "10 Effective Ways Intelligent People Deal with Rude People." Entrepreneur Legendary Network VIP.

12. Eric V. Copage, 1993, Black Pearls, Quell William Marrow, New York.

13. Elisa Morgan, 2021, "The Wisdom We Need," July 9, Our Daily Bread.

14. Evan Morgan, 2021, "Divinely Aligned." April 24, Our Daily Bread.

15. God's Wisdom for Today: My Daily Scripture Devotional, 2013. pp322, 345, 361, ThomasNelson.com

16. "Gratitude 101: A Gift We Give Ourselves." Day of Renewal Nursing Retreat.

17. Hannah Walt, 2013 "Surprising News about Anger." Prevention vol65: no6

18. Hitesh Bhasin, 2020, "The Meaning and Importance of respect." Marketing

19. J. Hampton, 2018. "The Relationship Between Sunshine, Serotonin, Vitamin D and Depression." The Best Brain Possible.

20. Jeff Herring, MS,LMFT. "Please Don't Panic: it's Time to Celebrate." http:www.tdo.com

21. Judith Orloff, MD, 2012, "The Power of Patience."

22. Karen Laing, 2013, "The Power of a Grateful Heart." Advance for Nurses. wwwAdvanceweb.com/nurses.

23. Life Application Study Bible; King James Version, 1996. Tyndale House Publisher Inc., Wheaton Illinois.

24. Linda C. Burton, 1997, "Stress management: Strategies, Tools, and Perspectives."

25. Lisa Sambra, 2021, "Never Alone," February 24, Our Daily Bread.

26. Moshe Ratson, MBA, MS, LML, 2017, The Value of Anger; 16 reasons it's good to get Angry." good therapy.org topic expert.

27. Petra Kolber, "Power of the Pause." Spryliving.com

28. "Respect: What is it: types, example, Learn and Teach."2019.

29. Richard Carlson, PHD, 1997, Don't Sweat the Small Stuff and it's all Small Stuff. Hyperion, New York.

30. Samuel Rodenhizer, 2020, "How do you Show Respect for Others," A Conscious Rethink.com.8558 respecting.

31. Sarah Mahoney, 2008, "But Everyone else is …." Family Circle.

32. Tim O'Brien, Tallahassee Democrat,"Set Goals to reach your Best,"; "Lighten Up, Laugh More," Live Longer," Don't Wait! Enjoy What you Have right Now,"; Do you Want Happiness? Take a Look Inside."

33. Webster's new Collegiate Dictionary, G and C Merrian Company, Springfield, Massachusetts.

34. Xochiti Dixon, 2021, "Two are Better," March 6, Our Daily Bread.

35. www.mindtools.com

About the Author

Gladys Wiggins, RN, MEd, MN is a retired Nursing Professor with two grandsons and one granddaughter. The youngest of these is fifteen years old. The inspiration to write came from her grandsons and a love of teaching and sharing inspirational messages. Additionally, the year 2020 was unlike any we have ever experienced. The pandemic limitations, racial issues, a divisive political climate, and law enforcement treatment of African Americans were some of the stress - producing happenings in society. All thing considered, writing allowed time to be used in a perceived constructive way that could have far reaching benefits.

The author has a passion for reality-based self-improvement and inspirational reading. Fictional readings are not as appreciated and enjoyable. The passion also extends to screen time. Viewing movies that deliver a message or evoke laughter are preferred. Collecting and saving workshop documents, newsletters, articles or nuggets that were inspirational through the years are now out of the file folder and being shared with others.

On January 6,2019, A sermon titled, "Intentional impact," was presented by her Pastor. He identified ways to affect our culture with Christ. Two ways were Christian Education and Strengthening the Family Nucleus. He emphasized "We cannot leave our children up to chance. We all have a part to play." This message was inspiring, stimulating, and motivating. It moved the author to challenge our youth to become better people by using intentional empowerment. While the target audience is young people, personal growth/development is important through all stages of life.

This tool may be useful in the psychological/emotional growth of youth and beyond. It may be instrumental in transforming ones' life. Becoming the best version of yourself takes work, time and consistency. Commit to be consistent and to invest in personal development which is a lifelong process. Prayerfully, this interactive book will be significant in changing the lives of youth in the Jacksonville community and beyond.

Tools to Enhance
Communication
and Progress

Thank You!

- ❏ Very thoughtful
- ❏ Very helpful to me
- ❏ Always willing to listen to any concern
- ❏ Acknowledged and congratulated me on achievements
- ❏ Very kindhearted and understanding
- ❏ Other

To:

From:

Date:

Note: _____

_____

_____

_____

_____

_____

_____

_____

_____

_____

_____

_____

FORGIVENESS

To:

From:

Date:

SUBJECT: I Forgive you

Re: _____

_____

_____

_____

_____

_____

_____

_____

_____

_____

_____

_____

_____

_____

_____

_____

_____

_____

_____

_____

_____

_____

_____

_____

_____

_____

_____

_____

_____

I Apologize

TO:

FROM:

RE:

I sincerely apologize for

_____

_____

_____

_____

_____

_____

_____

_____

_____

_____

_____

_____

_____

_____

_____

Please accept my apology.

Your friend,

SELF IMPROVEMENT ACTIVITY

My Strengths _____
_____
_____

    What I can do to strengthen my strong qualities _____
_____
_____

My Weaknesses _____
_____
_____

    What I can do to strengthen my weaknesses _____
_____
_____

Qualities I want to develop: _____
_____
_____

The one thing I would like to work on **improving** over the next four weeks is: _____
_____
_____

My short-term (6-12 months) self-improvement goal is: _____
_____

    Specific actions I will take to move toward reaching this goal are:_____
_____
_____

My long-term (12+ months) self-improvement goal is: _____
_____

    Specific actions I will take to move toward reaching this goal are: _____
_____
_____

RANDOM ACTS OF KINDNESS CALENDAR

PRACTICE PLANNED AND UNPLANNED ACTS OF KINDNESS 2-3 TIMES PER WEEK

Write your planned acts of kindness on the calendar at the beginning of the week

Sunday _____
_____
_____
_____

Monday _____
_____
_____
_____

Tuesday _____
_____
_____
_____

Wednesday _____
_____
_____
_____

Thursday _____
_____
_____
_____

Friday _____
_____
_____
_____

Saturday _____
_____
_____
_____

Duplicate this page as necessary

You
Are a
Great
Person
!

SOMETHING to CHEER ABOUT!

GREAT NEWS!

Special Message!

_____
_____
_____
_____
_____
_____
_____
_____
_____
_____
_____
_____
_____
_____
_____
_____
_____
_____
_____

From: ME
To: YOU

BECOMING the BEST VERSION of YOURSELF
using INTENTIONAL EMPOWERMENT
by Gladys Latimer Wiggins

To purchase this book, complete the order form.

Name _____

Organization _____

Mailing Address _____

City/State/Zip _____

Quantity Desired _____

Shipping and handling fee ($4.00)

Total amount enclosed _____
(Money order or personal check)

|||||||||||||||||||||||||||||||||||||||||||||||||||||||||||||||||||||||||||||||||||||||||||||||||||||||||||||||

Mail to: Gladys Wiggins

c/o RCSS

2255 Dunn Avenue

Suite 206

Jacksonville, Florida 32218

You may call (904) 264-5359 if you have questions.

Leave a message and your call will be returned within five (5) days.

You may also purchase from www.Amazon.com/shop/books